MW01703427

SRA

Specific Skill Series
for Language Arts

Sentences

Leveled Books
in Nine Key
Language Arts Skill Areas

SRA

Columbus, OH

The McGraw·Hill Companies

Cover: ©Tim Flach/Getty Images, Inc.

SRAonline.com

SRA

Send all inquiries to:
SRA/McGraw-Hill
8787 Orion Place
Columbus, OH 43240-4027

Printed in the United States of America.

ISBN 0-07-601706-0

3 4 5 6 7 8 9 RHR 14 13 12 11 10

TO THE TEACHER

GENERAL INFORMATION ON SENTENCES

Writing complete, effective sentences requires an understanding of grammar, word meaning, and the conventions of punctuation. Native speakers of English use correct sentences in speech from an early age, showing that they grasp the concept of a sentence, even if they have not yet learned to transform their speech into written sentences and to correctly mark sentence boundaries. Nonnative speakers, however, often lack a sense of the sound and structure of a sentence in English; they may require a greater amount of exposure, both audible and visual, before they can begin to write correct, complete sentences consistently.

Common errors in student writing, such as run-ons, fragments, and comma splices, often occur as young writers experiment with new structures that will allow them to express more complex ideas. Instruction in sentence combining helps developing writers use more complex sentence structures.

ABOUT *SPECIFIC SKILL SERIES FOR LANGUAGE ARTS*

Specific Skill Series for Language Arts is a companion to ***Specific Skill Series,*** a supplemental reading program that has been widely recognized for its effectiveness for over thirty years. The two series are designed and organized the same. ***Specific Skill Series for Language Arts*** consists of discrete units of practice exercises that target and reinforce fundamental language-arts skills. Units in both series are presented in multiple-choice format for standardized test practice.

ABOUT *SENTENCES*

The scope and sequence for Books A through H of *Sentences* focuses on the grammatical elements of a sentence, sentence combining, and common sentence problems. The scope and sequence for each book is located on the last page of the book. Each unit includes

- **rule boxes** that explain concepts and rules related to sentence writing.
- **models** in each rule box to illustrate the concepts and rules.
- **multiple-choice exercises** for skills practice and reinforcement.

Four **Language Activity Pages** (LAPs) appear in each book. Each LAP is divided into the following four sections and reviews the skills practiced in the preceding units:

Exercising Your Skill reviews key terms and concepts.
Expanding Your Skill provides mixed practice.
Exploring Language shows how the skills apply to real-world contexts by featuring one of six forms of writing: descriptive, narrative, personal, persuasive, expository, and poetry.
Expressing Yourself includes two creative activities related to the skills. One activity is always a Work-with-a-Partner activity to encourage collaborative learning.

TO THE TEACHER

SERIES COMPONENTS

- **Student Editions:** Nine books in each level (A–H) focus on nine skill areas: *Grammar, Usage, Mechanics, Spelling, Vocabulary, Sentences, Paragraphs, Writing Process,* and *Research.*
- **Placement Test Books:** One book for each skill area includes diagnostic tests to place students in the correct level.
- **Teacher's Manual:** Primarily an answer key, the *Teacher's Manual* also includes reproducible student worksheets and further information on how to use the program, including classroom management tips.

HOW TO USE *SPECIFIC SKILL SERIES FOR LANGUAGE ARTS*

Placing Students in Levels: The scope and sequence, complexity of skills, and readability in Levels A through H correspond to Grades 1 through 8. Students may, however, be placed in any level. For example, in the second grade, a student who needs remedial work in a specific skill may be placed in Book A, an on-level student who would benefit from skills reinforcement may be placed in Book B, and an advanced student who is ready for enrichment may be placed in Book C or higher. *Placement Tests* help place students in the correct level.

Setting: This series can be used for independent study and one-on-one practice sessions, as well as in small-group and whole-class settings. It is also effective in after-school and summer-school programs.

Getting Started: Students must have notebook paper or copies of reproducible student worksheets (located in the *Teacher's Manual*) before they begin working. Remind students not to write in the books. Students may begin in any unit of any book, depending on the skill practice they need, although it is recommended that they begin with Unit 1. As they work through the units, students should record their answers on notebook paper or on the student worksheets.

Pacing: Students should be encouraged to work at their own pace, completing a few units every day or every other day.

Scoring: Teachers should score units as soon as they have been completed. Then a discussion can be held in which students justify their answer choices.

Internet Use: Some activities, especially those in *Research,* require students to use the Internet. Students' use of the Internet should be monitored closely for content appropriateness and safety.

TO THE STUDENT

Although you use sentences constantly when you speak and write, it is easy to make mistakes because there are so many rules for writing correct, complete sentences. This book will help you make fewer mistakes in your speech and written work.

In Book E *Sentences,* you will learn about

- Building Sentences
- Combining Sentences
- The Sound of Language
- Sentence Fluency
- Parallelism
- Sentence Problems
- Expanding Sentences

After you complete this book, you will be able to combine several sentences into one sentence that keeps the original meaning and is more fluent and interesting.

The dog has short fur. The dog has silky fur. The dog is brown.

Good: The dog has short, silky fur that is brown.

Better: The brown dog has short, silky fur.

You will also learn to expand sentences by adding details to them. Two ways to do this are to add a participial phrase or an appositive phrase.

Adding a Participial Phrase

The tea will taste great chilled. ⟶

The tea **soaking in the sun** will taste great chilled.

Adding an Appositive Phrase

Nebo is inland. ⟶

Nebo, **a town in North Carolina,** is inland.

By mastering the skills in this book, you will know whether or not a sentence is complete and correctly punctuated. You will also know how to improve your sentences, which will improve your writing.

Unit 1
Building Sentences

Simple Subjects and Predicates

A complete sentence includes a **subject** and a **predicate.** The subject tells *whom* or *what* the sentence is about. The predicate tells what the subject *does, is,* or *has.*

Water gushed from the fountain.

SUBJECT PREDICATE

- A **simple subject** is the noun or pronoun that performs the action of a sentence. It tells what the sentence is about.
- A **simple predicate** is the verb that expresses the action or state of being in a sentence. The simple predicate can also be a **verb phrase,** which includes a main verb and all of its helping verbs.

An arctic **fox hid** in that cave.

SIMPLE SUBJECT SIMPLE PREDICATE

Fluid Fire

Choose the simple subject or simple predicate that best completes each sentence.

1. The volcano ________ suddenly.
PREDICATE
(A) lava (B) rock (C) erupted

2. Lava ________ all around the volcano.
PREDICATE
(A) ground (B) oozes (C) hot

3. ________ of liquid rock create bright orange pathways.
SUBJECT
(A) Breaking (B) Roll (C) Streams

4. The pathways ________ most of what they touch.
PREDICATE
(A) melt (B) mountain (C) cools

5. Fortunately, the ________ is in a remote area.
SUBJECT
(A) stays (B) wind (C) volcano

Unit 1
Building Sentences

Choose the simple subject or simple predicate that best completes each sentence.

A Mobile Home

(6) Hermit crabs _____ crustaceans, or animals with a soft body inside of a hard body. (7) A hermit crab's _____ is unprotected. (8) Therefore, the hermit crab must _____ for a very safe dwelling. (9) Hermit crabs usually _____ into an empty shell of their size. (10) This new _____ shelters the hermit crab until it grows too large. (11) Once a hermit crab outgrows a shell, _____ will hunt for an even bigger house.

6. **(A)** are **(B)** gets **(C)** be

7. **(A)** belly **(B)** eyes **(C)** weak

8. **(A)** sand **(B)** search **(C)** rents

9. **(A)** crawl **(B)** sleeping **(C)** snails

10. **(A)** moved **(B)** claws **(C)** home

11. **(A)** we **(B)** adult **(C)** it

America's Dairyland

(12) "America's Dairyland" _____ one of the mottos that represents the state of Wisconsin. (13) _____ refers to things like milk, butter, and cheese. (14) Many _____ of Wisconsin provide a vast quantity of dairy products to the country. (15) They _____ a lot of help though. (16) Without cows, one state _____ would have to be replaced.

12. **(A)** mark **(B)** are **(C)** is

13. **(A)** Mottos **(B)** Dairy **(C)** Hill

14. **(A)** place **(B)** people **(C)** tours

15. **(A)** have **(B)** start **(C)** has

16. **(A)** tree **(B)** flowers **(C)** motto

Unit 2

Building Sentences

Complete Subjects and Predicates

Sentences can be broken into complete subjects and complete predicates.

- A sentence's **complete subject** includes the simple subject and any words that describe it.

  The motorcycle in the garage needs minor repairs.

- A sentence's **complete predicate** includes the simple predicate and any words that complete its meaning.

  By next week, the motorcycle **will be fixed**.

Match each complete subject with its correct complete predicate.

Complete Subject	Complete Predicate
1. Our school's trampoline	(A) can protect eyes from the sun.
2. Those bricks	(B) gave the skaters high scores.
3. The airplane on the runway	(C) received permission for takeoff.
4. The arctic hare	(D) does not have laces.
5. A broken door	(E) is now advertised for a cheaper price.
6. My dad's recipe	(F) is surrounded by a safety net and mats.
7. Special sunglasses	(G) is listed as a fire hazard.
8. Every judge at the competition	(H) calls for one cup of flour.
9. The shoe in this box	(I) support her ankles well.
10. Your new car	(J) will be used in the shed's foundation.
11. The library book	(K) has been checked out again.
12. Toni's rollerblades	(L) can change its fur color.

Unit 2
Building Sentences

Complete Subject	Complete Predicate
13. A huge network called the Internet	(A) can last a few weeks.
14. The Greek city of Athens	(B) live at the city zoo.
15. Flowering plants	(C) has been lost at the airport.
16. Our recycling bins	(D) connects computers around the world.
17. The camping store	(E) are typically tall with hourly chimes.
18. Animals from all over the world	(F) contain cans and bottles.
19. The common cold	(G) translates English into Spanish.
20. My mom's suitcase	(H) can reproduce by forming seeds.
21. Immigrants from many countries	(I) have easily recognized feathers.
22. Colorful parrots	(J) was mailed from Connecticut.
23. This letter from Alex	(K) have been renovated.
24. The weekend's practice schedule	(L) is to find alike pairs.
25. These old apartments	(M) was posted outside of the gym.
26. This language Web site	(N) is named for the goddess Athena.
27. Grandfather clocks	(O) brought new cultures to the United States.
28. The goal of the game	(P) is where we bought our tent.

Unit 2

Building Sentences

- In a sentence, do *not* mistake a subordinate, or dependent, clause for a complete subject or a complete predicate even though it has its own subject and predicate. A subordinate clause can be *part of* a complete subject or predicate, but it cannot stand alone as one or the other.

Today's chores | will not begin **until you have eaten lunch.**

COMPLETE SUBJECT — COMPLETE PREDICATE

- A participial phrase cannot be a complete subject or predicate either. Participial phrases begin with a verb form, but they usually describe something in the sentence and cannot stand alone.

Standing by a tree, the deer | nibbles on some wildflowers.

COMPLETE SUBJECT — COMPLETE PREDICATE

Choose the complete subject or complete predicate that correctly completes each sentence.

29. _____ are too wet to play on since it rained.

(A) Playing on the court,
(B) Outside
(C) The tennis courts

30. Her sprained ankle _____.

(A) does not require her to use crutches
(B) does not require
(C) while waiting for a bus

31. _____ was rescued near a sewer.

(A) Animals
(B) Carlisle's pet turtle
(C) Behind the house

32. _____ replaces yesterday's work.

(A) After school
(B) Our new assignment
(C) Teachers

Unit 2
Building Sentences

33. An association of chefs _____.
(A) is visiting for a local conference
(B) throughout the weekend
(C) stirring the soup

---

34. _____ is for advanced artists.
(A) The painting course
(B) Wishing I was enrolled,
(C) Art classes

---

35. Several movies _____.
(A) and been previewed
(B) ruining their endings
(C) have been added to his gift list

---

36. Debate team members _____.
(A) excited about the tournament
(B) will compete next month
(C) competing to be in the finals

---

37. _____ was crying because she had a fever.
(A) Moving in her crib
(B) Her parents
(C) The fussy baby

---

38. _____ is too tall for this table.
(A) Under the chair
(B) Knees
(C) My desk chair

---

39. _____ work different shifts at Lawson Hospital.
(A) Volunteer nurses
(B) That doctor
(C) Within the building

---

40. A car's license plates _____.
(A) glaring in the sun
(B) help to identify the owner
(C) but is not always on the front and back

Unit 3

Building Sentences

Compound Subjects and Predicates

Sentences can have more than one subject or predicate.

- A **compound subject** is two or more simple subjects that share the same verb. Compound subjects can be connected by *and* or *or.*

  Fruit or yogurt is the snack I prefer.

- A **compound predicate** is two or more simple predicates (verbs) that share the same subject. Compound predicates can be connected by *and, but,* or *or.*

  Meteorologists **observe and predict** weather conditions.

Choose the compound subject or compound predicate that correctly completes each sentence.

1. _____ are featured on the American flag.
   (A) The stars of the states
   (B) Stars and stripes
   (C) Stripes

---

2. The sandwich _____ in the oven.
   (A) bakes and toasts
   (B) toasts
   (C) baking

---

3. Our class _____ with the sound of a bell.
   (A) ends
   (B) begins after I hear
   (C) begins and ends

---

4. _____ left these webbed tracks.
   (A) Geese
   (B) Ducks from that pond
   (C) Ducks or geese

---

5. Sun Yi _____ her teeth every night before going to sleep.
   (A) brushes and flosses
   (B) brushes
   (C) flosses in front of a mirror

6. The divers _____ to locate the ship's anchor.
(A) tried but failed
(B) tried in the dark
(C) failed in the dark

7. Janelle _____ eggs for breakfast.
(A) scrambling
(B) scrambles or fries
(C) fries in a pan

8. _____ require flexibility.
(A) Dancing
(B) Sports with a partner
(C) Dancing and sports

9. _____ will ask more questions to complete the article.
(A) A reporter or a columnist
(B) A local reporter
(C) This week's columnist

10. _____ can pose a threat to the environment.
(A) Chemical waste
(B) Oil and chemicals
(C) Spilled oil

11. That bluejay _____ a worm.
(A) grabbed but dropped
(B) dropped from his beak
(C) grabs

12. _____ completed the extra-credit project.
(A) Henry and Katherine
(B) Henry's classmate
(C) Katherine in the morning class

Unit 3
Building Sentences

When there are more than two subjects in a compound subject or more than two verbs in a compound predicate, use commas to separate them.

- Place a comma after each subject except for the last one.
  Marge, Mae, and Mabel are my horses.
- Place a comma after each verb except for the last one.
  My horses **eat, rest, and run** in the same field.

Choose the compound subject or compound predicate that correctly completes each sentence.

13. _____ hang in the closet.
    (A) Coats, or shirts
    (B) The pants that do not fit
    (C) Coats, shirts, and pants

14. Edward _____ at his desk.
    (A) reads, studies, draws, and writes
    (B) draws storybook characters
    (C) reads, and writes

15. _____ are fragile crafts.
    (A) Glass, ceramics, and dried flowers
    (B) Glass, ceramics
    (C) Glass, and ceramics

16. Birds _____ to get where they are going.
    (A) hop, and fly
    (B) fly, hop, or walk
    (C) fly hop or walk

17. That train _____ before it reached the crossing.
    (A) needed repairs
    (B) started, slowed, and stopped
    (C) started, or stopped

18. _____ is going to be my autumn activity.
(A) Wrestling, football, or basketball
(B) Wrestling or, basketball
(C) The sports

---

19. _____ are completing one science project together.
(A) Felipe's idea
(B) A student in this class
(C) John, Felipe, and Brad

---

20. The family _____ its model car collection.
(A) owns
(B) finds, organizes, and displays
(C) cleaning in the attic

---

21. _____ can be tasty dessert decorations.
(A) Frosting, sprinkles, and candy
(B) Baking dishes
(C) A delightful cake

---

22. Some animals _____ their winter food.
(A) searching for
(B) search for, gather, and store
(C) gather, or, store

---

23. Elise _____ the baseball.
(A) grabbing for
(B) throwing quickly
(C) grabs for, catches, and throws

---

24. _____ were the first guests to arrive at the family picnic.
(A) This Sunday's weather
(B) Among the cousins
(C) Travis, Jocelyn, Max, and Andre

Unit 4
Building Sentences

Compound Sentences

A **compound sentence** is made of two or more simple sentences, which are joined by a comma (,) and a conjunction *(and, but, or),* or a semicolon (;). When a semicolon is used, do *not* use a coordinating conjunction.

I put sunscreen on my face, **but** my freckles appeared anyway.

Freckles are small**;** sometimes they overlap and look larger.

Face It

What is the correct way to write each compound sentence?

1. **(A)** Eyebrows are very expressive; they can show surprise or anger.
   (B) Eyebrows are very expressive and they can show surprise or anger.
   (C) Eyebrows are very expressive; and can show surprise or anger.

---

2. **(A)** Some dimples are always there but others show up only when someone smiles.
   (B) Some dimples are always there and; others show up only when someone smiles.
   (C) Some dimples are always there, and others show up only when someone smiles.

---

3. **(A)** Noses change throughout a person's life; and they usually get wider instead of longer.
   (B) Noses change throughout a person's life; they usually get wider instead of longer.
   (C) Noses change throughout a person's life or they usually get wider instead of longer.

---

4. **(A)** It is very rare but some people have two different-colored eyes.
   (B) It is very rare, but some people have two different-colored eyes.
   (C) It is very rare; but some people have two different-colored eyes.

---

5. **(A)** Humans are the only animals that blush, and they cannot control it.
   (B) Humans are the only animals that blush and they cannot control it.
   (C) Humans are the only animals that blush, and, they cannot control it.

Unit 4
Building Sentences

America's Last Frontier

6. **(A)** Alaska was a Russian colony but the United States bought it.
   (B) Alaska was a Russian colony, but the United States bought it.
   (C) Alaska was a Russian colony; but the United States bought it.

7. **(A)** Alaska was purchased in 1867, but, it was not a state until 1959.
   (B) Alaska was purchased in 1867 but it was not a state until 1959.
   (C) Alaska was purchased in 1867, but it was not a state until 1959.

8. **(A)** Joe Juneau discovered gold in Alaska and; the state capital is named after him.
   (B) Joe Juneau discovered gold in Alaska, the state capital is named after him.
   (C) Joe Juneau discovered gold in Alaska; the state capital is named after him.

9. **(A)** Hikers climb Mt. McKinley, or they explore Chugach State Park.
   (B) Hikers climb Mt. McKinley or they explore Chugach State Park.
   (C) Hikers climb Mt. McKinley; or they explore Chugach State Park.

10. **(A)** Alaska is the largest of the United States; it is twice the size of Texas.
    (B) Alaska is the largest of the United States, it is twice the size of Texas.
    (C) Alaska is the largest of the United States and it is twice the size of Texas.

11. **(A)** Alaska's record high was 100° F and its record low was -80° F.
    (B) Alaska's record high was 100° F, and its record low was -80° F.
    (C) Alaska's record high was 100° F; and its record low was -80° F.

12. **(A)** Juneau is Alaska's capital; but Anchorage is its largest city.
    (B) Juneau is Alaska's capital, but Anchorage is its largest city.
    (C) Juneau is Alaska's capital but Anchorage is its largest city.

Unit 4

Building Sentences

Complex Sentences

A **complex sentence** is made of one independent clause and one or more dependent clauses. An independent clause can stand on its own as a sentence. A dependent clause cannot stand on its own, even though it has a subject and a predicate. Dependent clauses begin with a subordinating conjunction, such as *although, before, unless,* and *while.*

I read near a light source | where it is easier to see.

INDEPENDENT CLAUSE | DEPENDENT CLAUSE

However, when a complex sentence begins with a dependent clause, place a comma after it.

Whenever I start a new book, I make my own bookmark.

Fire Safety

Choose the correct clause to build a complex sentence.

13. _____ you need to remain calm.
    (A) Whenever possible,
    (B) In an emergency,
    (C) When there is a fire,

---

14. Feel doors with the back of your hand _____.
    (A) before you open them
    (B) instead of your palm
    (C) quickly and lightly

---

15. Cracks around doors should be sealed with damp towels _____.
    (A) until firefighters arrive
    (B) or duct tape
    (C) from the bathroom or the kitchen

---

16. _____ the wrong kind can make a fire worse.
    (A) Even after an inspection,
    (B) Though fire extinguishers are useful,
    (C) In an attic or a basement,

Unit 4
Building Sentences

17. Unusual odors might be noticed _____.
(A) by animals
(B) around household equipment
(C) before an electrical fire ignites

---

18. _____ it is important to have an emergency plan.
(A) Now and then,
(B) Because fires spread swiftly,
(C) For every building,

---

19. Your family should choose a place _____.
(A) where you all can meet
(B) in the neighborhood
(C) and a time to practice

---

20. _____ ask a neighbor to call 911.
(A) Politely but firmly
(B) Immediately after,
(C) Once you are safe from harm,

---

21. You should sleep with your door closed _____.
(A) at all times
(B) in case of a fire
(C) because it holds back heat and smoke

---

22. _____ many homes still do not have them.
(A) Near the kitchen and in every bedroom,
(B) Although most people know about smoke detectors,
(C) Surprisingly enough,

---

23. Unless there is access to a fire escape, _____.
(A) steadily with a water hose
(B) in an elevator
(C) keep a rope ladder on upstairs levels

Unit 4
Building Sentences

Compound-Complex Sentences

A **compound-complex sentence** is made of more than one independent clause and at least one dependent clause. Remember that a dependent clause has a subject and a predicate but cannot stand alone. In the model below, the dependent clause is boldfaced.

Fifty-five million people reside in Ethiopia, **where drought is a continual threat,** and most of them live on small family farms.

Around Africa

Choose the correct clause to build a compound-complex sentence.

24. Because two branches of the Nile River meet in central Sudan, this region of the country is very fertile, _____.

(A) and huge fields of cotton grow there
(B) although drought occurred in the 1990s
(C) but must be maintained

---

25. _____ but most of the country lies on the mainland, where Kilimanjaro is located.

(A) Tanzania includes several islands,
(B) Tanzania's largest island,
(C) With a coastline of beautiful white beaches,

---

26. Kilimanjaro is Africa's tallest mountain, _____, though its last eruption happened more than 100,000 years ago.

(A) with many other names
(B) but it is also a volcano
(C) in smaller volcanoes nearby

---

27. _____ mountain climbers face overwhelming challenges, and many will not succeed.

(A) Overlooking endless plains,
(B) Risky and ready to make an attempt,
(C) Because Kilimanjaro stands an imposing 19,340 feet,

Unit 4
Building Sentences

28. The Belgian Congo changed its name after it became independent, _____.
(A) separating from Belgium
(B) once and for all
(C) and the country is now called the Democratic Republic of Congo

---

29. The people of Nigeria speak many different African languages, _____ when they conduct business.
(A) but most Nigerians use English
(B) which is confusing
(C) but not

---

30. Although the equator crosses southern Uganda, its high elevations keep temperatures mild, _____.
(A) for East Africa
(B) which helps crops grow well
(C) and the annual rainfall is ample

---

31. _____ that was founded by freed slaves, and the capital city of Monrovia was named after United States president James Monroe.
(A) A country on Africa's west coast
(B) Liberia is a West African country
(C) Like its neighbor Sierra Leone

---

32. When black South Africans voted for the first time in 1994, they elected Nelson Mandela, _____.
(A) freed from prison
(B) winner of the Nobel Peace Prize
(C) and he became the country's first black president

---

33. Mining provides most of Zimbabwe's income, _____ where they grow corn and raise cattle.
(A) from gold and copper mines
(B) but the majority of its residents work on farms,
(C) especially in areas

---

34. Kenya is in Africa, and its coast is on the Indian Ocean _____.
(A) whereas Lake Rudolf is inland
(B) many wild animals
(C) close to the southern tip of Africa

The First LAP
Language Activity Pages

A. Exercising Your Skill

You have been learning about simple, complete, and compound subjects and predicates. You have also learned about compound, complex, and compound-complex sentences. Number your paper from 1 to 5. Read the sentences below. Use a word from the box only once to complete each sentence correctly.

conjunction	Subordinate	semicolon	Compound	Complete

1. _____ subjects and predicates include all words that describe them.
2. _____ subjects and predicates include more than one subject and predicate.
3. _____ clauses can be part of complete subjects or predicates.
4. A comma and a _____ can be used to join two simple sentences.
5. In a compound sentence, a _____ is not used with a coordinating conjunction.

B. Expanding Your Skill

Number your paper from 1 to 10. Read the sentences below. Decide if each underlined part is a subject or a predicate. Then decide if it is complete or compound. For each complete subject, write **CES** on your paper. For each complete predicate, write **CEP.** For each compound subject, write **CDS.** For each compound predicate, write **CDP.**

1. Waking from a dream, I tossed and turned in my bed.
2. The dream that woke me showed my family in miniature form.
3. My aunt, uncle, and cousin from down the street were in my dream.
4. Plump, giant balloons grew on trees in my dream.
5. Floating in the air, the balloons would carry butterflies with them.
6. If the balloons popped, flowers trickled and tumbled out of them.
7. Waterfalls and raindrops in my dream were various colors.
8. The red raindrops in my dream tasted like strawberries.
9. My mom, dad, brother, and dog lived in a miniature house.
10. We danced, sang, worked, slept, and ate in our mini home.

C. Exploring Language

Descriptive Writing Number your paper from 1 to 5. Read the passage below to decide which five sentences are complex sentences. Write the letters of those sentences on your paper.

(A) A mongoose is a small land animal that is related to weasels. (B) Mongoose species inhabit areas that range from Africa to parts of South Asia. (C) One species has even been traced to southern Spain. (D) Mongooses are known as very effective snake hunters, and most become active at night. (E) Some mongoose species include banded, dwarf, hornbill, slender, and marsh. (F) Banded mongooses seem to be the most social because they live in groups of up to forty members. (G) Dwarf and hornbill mongooses live in underground burrows in manageable family units, which include eight members on average. (H) Mongooses can also make their homes in abandoned holes or rock crevices. (I) Slender mongooses are active day and night and have sleek coats, long bodies, and black-tipped tails. (J) Marsh mongooses live near rivers and swamps probably because they enjoy eating mollusks and crabs. (K) Unlike slender mongooses, marsh mongooses have shaggy coats. (L) Including the tail, many mongoose species can measure up to four feet long.

D. Expressing Yourself

Choose one of these activities. When you are finished, give your paper to your teacher.

1. Select a brief article to cut out of a newspaper or a magazine. If you get an article at a library, photocopy it instead of cutting it out. In the article, find at least one example of the following sentence types: compound, complex, and compound-complex. Highlight the examples in the article, or write them on a separate sheet of paper. If you notice more than one of each, feel free to highlight or write those as well.

2. WORK with a PARTNER With a partner, write three complex sentences and two compound-complex sentences. When you are finished, you should have a total of five sentences. Take turns writing the independent and dependent clauses that are necessary to build each sentence type. If it helps, write your sentences based on a theme.

Unit 5

Combining Sentences

Combining with Subjects and Predicates

Simple, related sentences can be combined to avoid repetition and to make them sound better. One way to do this is to combine subjects. Correctly use *and* or *or* to combine more than one subject.

Nerves are just beneath the skin. Blood vessels are just beneath the skin.

Nerves and blood vessels are just beneath the skin.

A papercut left this scar. A scratch left this scar.

A papercut or a scratch left this scar.

- Another way to join simple sentences is to combine predicates. Correctly use *and, but,* or *or* to combine more than one predicate.

Skin produces cells constantly. Skin loses cells constantly.

Skin **produces and loses** cells constantly.

Skin stretches its shape. Skin maintains its shape.

Skin **stretches but maintains** its shape.

Remember that the newly combined sentence should have the same meaning or share the same idea as the previous shorter sentences.

Marvelous Muscles

What is the best way to combine each sentence pair?

1. A muscle can contract. A muscle can relax.
   (A) A muscle can contract, and it can relax.
   (B) A muscle can contract and relax.
   (C) A muscle can contract, and a muscle can relax.

2. Without a warm-up, muscles can be stressed. Muscles can be pulled.
   (A) Without a warm-up, muscles can be stressed or pulled.
   (B) Without a warm-up, muscles can be stressed, or they can be pulled.
   (C) Without a warm-up, muscles can be stressed or can be pulled.

3. Face muscles allow you to smile. Face muscles allow you to frown.
   (A) Face muscles allow you to smile, and they allow you to frown.
   (B) The muscles in your face allow you to smile and frown.
   (C) Face muscles allow you to smile and frown.

Unit 5
Combining Sentences

When more than one subject has been combined, remember that the verb must agree in number.

- For subjects joined by *and,* use the plural verb form most of the time.
  Incorrect: Nails and hair **grows**.
  Correct: Nails and hair **grow**.
- For subjects joined by *or,* the verb should agree with the subject closest to it.
  Incorrect: A fracture or a break **are** in my thumb.
  Correct: A fracture or a break **is** in my thumb.

What is the best way to combine each sentence pair?

4. Biking develops quadriceps. Running develops quadriceps.
   (A) Biking, running develop quadriceps.
   (B) Biking develops and running develops quadriceps.
   (C) Biking and running develop quadriceps.

5. Unexercised muscles become weaker. They become smaller.
   (A) Unexercised muscles become weaker and smaller.
   (B) Unexercised muscles become weaker, and they become smaller.
   (C) Unexercised muscles become weaker, and muscles become smaller.

6. Freckles increase with sun exposure. Pigment increases with sun exposure.
   (A) Freckles or pigment increase with sun exposure.
   (B) Freckles or pigment increases with sun exposure.
   (C) Freckles or pigment can increase with sun exposure.

7. The brain controls our body. The brain controls our functions.
   (A) The brain controls our body, or it controls our functions.
   (B) The brain controls our body and functions.
   (C) The brain control body functions.

8. A strained muscle might be tender. A strained muscle might be bruised.
   (A) A strained muscle might be tender and bruised.
   (B) A strained muscle might be tender, and it might be bruised.
   (C) A strained muscle might be tender, and a muscle is bruised.

Unit 5

Combining Sentences

Combining with Adjectives and Adverbs

Adjectives that describe the same thing in different sentences can be combined. Make sure it is clear which noun the adjectives describe in the newly combined sentence.

That piece of gold is shiny. That piece of gold is lumpy.

That piece of gold is **shiny and lumpy**.

Adverbs that describe the same action in different sentences can be combined. Though an adverb does *not* have a fixed location in a sentence, it should be clear which verb the adverb is describing.

The gold was packed gently. The gold was packed quickly.

The gold was packed **gently but quickly**.

What is the best way to combine each sentence pair?

9. The Gold Rush was a long journey for many. The journey was difficult.

(A) The Gold Rush was a long journey, but not difficult for many.
(B) The difficult Gold Rush was a long journey for many.
(C) The Gold Rush was a long and difficult journey for many.

---

10. Communities sprang up instantly. They sprang up cooperatively.

(A) Communities sprang up instantly and cooperatively.
(B) Cooperative communities sprang up instantly.
(C) Communities sprang up instantly with cooperation.

---

11. Gold miners searched rivers endlessly. They searched desperately.

(A) Gold miners desperately searched endless rivers.
(B) Endless gold miners searched rivers desperately.
(C) Gold miners searched rivers endlessly and desperately.

---

12. Some people spent their wealth hastily. Some spent it foolishly.

(A) Some people spent their wealth hastily and foolishly.
(B) Foolish people spent some of their wealth hastily.
(C) Some hasty people spent their wealth foolishly.

---

13. The Gold Rush had an important effect. It was a lasting effect.

(A) The Gold Rush had a last, important effect.
(B) The Gold Rush had an important and a lasting effect.
(C) The important effect of the Gold Rush was lasting.

Unit 5
Combining Sentences

Combining with Prepositional Phrases

Prepositional phrases that refer to the same word in different but related sentences can be combined. It should be clear to what or whom they refer.

Grapes withered on vines. Grapes withered under the sun.

Grapes withered **on vines under the sun**.

What is the best way to combine each sentence pair?

14. Palm trees grow in warm climates. Palm trees grow on several islands.
(A) Palm trees grow in warm climates, and they grow on several islands.
(B) Palm trees grow in warm climates on several islands.
(C) Palm trees grow in warm climates, and they are on islands.

15. Trains rumble along these tracks. The tracks are under an old wooden bridge.
(A) Trains rumble along under the tracks of an old wooden bridge.
(B) Trains rumble along the tracks of an old wooden bridge.
(C) Trains rumble along these tracks under an old wooden bridge.

16. Squirrels scurried to the acorns. Squirrels scurried near the tree.
(A) Squirrels scurried to the acorns, and they were near the tree.
(B) Squirrels scurried to the acorns near the tree.
(C) Squirrels scurried to the tree's acorns.

17. Much of the land is used for farming. The land is in the Midwest.
(A) Much of the land is used for farming in the Midwest.
(B) Much of the Midwest is used for farming.
(C) Much of the farming land is in the Midwest.

18. Corrin pressed a daisy between the pages. They were the pages of her favorite book.

(A) Corrin pressed a daisy between her favorite books.
(B) Corrin pressed a daisy between the pages, and the daisy was pressed in her favorite book.
(C) Corrin pressed a daisy between the pages of her favorite book.

Unit 6

Combining Sentences

Combining with Appositives and Appositive Phrases

An **appositive** is a noun that is located next to another noun which it describes or adds information about. An appositive from one sentence can be added to another sentence when both sentences describe the same noun. Use commas to set off an appositive if it is *not* needed to complete the meaning of the sentence.

Brazil's capital is a spectacular place. Brazil's capital is Brasilia.

Brazil's capital, **Brasilia,** is a spectacular place.

An **appositive phrase** includes the appositive and the other words that modify or describe it. Like an appositive, an appositive phrase always appears next to the noun it describes. It is usually set off by commas.

Rio de Janeiro is on the eastern coast. It was once Brazil's capital.

Rio de Janeiro, **once Brazil's capital,** is on the eastern coast.

What is the best way to combine each sentence pair, using an appositive or an appositive phrase?

1. Martha Washington's husband was the first United States president. Martha Washington's husband was George.
   (A) Martha Washington's husband, George, was the first United States president.
   (B) Martha Washington's husband, and the first president of the United States, was George.
   (C) George was Martha Washington's husband, and the first president of the United States.

---

2. The bouzouki is a stringed instrument. It is Greek in origin.
   (A) The bouzouki, a stringed instrument with a Greek origin.
   (B) The bouzouki is a stringed instrument that is Greek in origin.
   (C) The bouzouki, a stringed instrument, is Greek in origin.

---

3. The Everglades is a national park. The Everglades National Park is mainly swampland.
   (A) The Everglades, a national park, is mainly swampland.
   (B) Mainly swampland, the Everglades is a national park.
   (C) The Everglades is mainly swampland, a national park.

4. Gumbo is a spicy stew of meat, seafood, and vegetables. Gumbo is a popular dish in Louisiana.
   (A) Gumbo is a popular dish in Louisiana, a spicy stew of meat, seafood, and vegetables.
   (B) Gumbo, a popular dish in Louisiana, is a spicy stew of meat, seafood, and vegetables.
   (C) Gumbo, a popular and spicy stew of meat, seafood, and vegetables, is a dish in Louisiana.

5. The North Star is also known as Polaris. It can be used by sailors to navigate their voyages.
   (A) The North Star is also known as Polaris and has guided sailors as they navigate their voyages.
   (B) The North Star, Polaris, can be used by sailors to navigate their voyages.
   (C) Polaris can be used by sailors to navigate their voyages.

6. Elephants are a type of pachyderm. Pachyderms have very thick skin.
   (A) Elephants are pachyderms with very thick skin.
   (B) Elephants, with very thick skin, are pachyderms.
   (C) Elephants, a type of pachyderm, have very thick skin.

7. Ellen Ochoa is an astronaut. Ellen Ochoa studied at Stanford University.
   (A) Astronaut Ellen Ochoa studied at Stanford University.
   (B) Ellen Ochoa at Stanford University, studied to be an astronaut.
   (C) Ellen Ochoa, an astronaut, studied at Stanford University.

8. Plexiglass is a hard plastic that is typically transparent like glass. Plexiglass is a durable material.
   (A) Plexiglass, a durable material, is a hard plastic that is typically transparent like glass.
   (B) Plexiglass is a hard plastic that is typically transparent like glass, and durable.
   (C) Plexiglass is a durable, hard plastic that is typically transparent like glass.

Unit 6
Combining Sentences

Combining with Participles and Participial Phrases

A **participle** is a verb form that can act as an adjective to describe a noun or a pronoun. A participle is often formed by adding *-ed* or *-ing* to a verb. A participle from one sentence can be added to another sentence to describe the related noun or pronoun.

The bird escaped the storm. The bird was frightened.

The **frightened** bird escaped the storm.

A **participial phrase** includes the participle and the other words to complete its meaning. To form a participial phrase when combining two related sentences, you may have to add *-ed* or *-ing* to the appropriate verb. Then leave out its complete subject. Use a comma after a participial phrase when it occurs at the beginning of a sentence.

The cat leaped onto the windowsill. The cat watched birds fly.

Leaping onto the windowsill, the cat watched birds fly.

What is the best way to combine each sentence pair, using a participle or a participial phrase?

9. The lighthouse guides us home. The lighthouse gleams in the night.
(A) Gleaming in the night, the lighthouse guides us home.
(B) The lighthouse was gleaming and, in the night, guides us home.
(C) The lighthouse in the night, guides us home gleaming.

---

10. The potatoes and carrots taste delicious. The potatoes and carrots are roasted.
(A) The roasted potatoes and carrots taste delicious.
(B) The potatoes and roasted carrots taste delicious.
(C) Tasting delicious are the roasted potatoes and carrots.

---

11. Becca felt a pain in her head. The pain was throbbing.
(A) Becca felt a pain in her throbbing head.
(B) Becca felt a pain, throbbing, that was in her head.
(C) Becca felt a throbbing pain in her head.

---

12. The team had a winning season. They were inspired by the coach.
(A) Inspired by a winning season, the team had a coach.
(B) Inspired by the coach, the team had a winning season.
(C) Having a winning season, the coach inspired the team.

13. The group of tourists hiked one of the Grand Canyon's trails. The group of tourists was excited.
   (A) The group of tourists hiked with excitement on one of the Grand Canyon's trails.
   (B) Grouping of tourists, they hiked excitedly on one of the Grand Canyon's trails.
   (C) The excited group of tourists hiked one of the Grand Canyon's trails.

---

14. The mountains near the Danube River are dazzling. The mountains rise from the ground.
   (A) Rising from the ground, the mountains near the Danube River are dazzling.
   (B) Dazzle, mountains near the Danube River rise from the ground.
   (C) Nearing the Danube River, dazzling mountains rise from the ground.

---

15. The judge listened carefully to determine the facts of the case. The judge was experienced.
   (A) The judge listened carefully, but was determined about the facts.
   (B) The experienced judge listened carefully to determine the facts of the case.
   (C) Determined to listen carefully, the experienced judge heard the case's facts.

---

16. The fish hide among the coral. The fish are threatened.
   (A) The fish hide among the coral, threatened.
   (B) Threatening the coral, the fish hide.
   (C) The threatened fish hide among the coral.

---

17. The Channel Tunnel is an engineering marvel. The Channel Tunnel extends underwater between England and France.
   (A) The Channel Tunnel extends underwater between England and France and is an engineering marvel.
   (B) Extending underwater between England and France, the Channel Tunnel is an engineering marvel.
   (C) Between England and France is an underwater engineering marvel, the Channel Tunnel.

Unit 6

Combining Sentences

Combining Parts from Three Sentences

When there are two or more sentences that have information referring to the same thing, sometimes the related parts of each sentence can be combined into one sentence. Remember that one goal of combining sentences is to make them sound better. Each sentence part should be placed correctly in the new sentence so that the meaning of the original sentences is not changed or lost.

The artist mixed paints. He mixed the paints on the palette. He held the palette in his hand.

Incorrect: The artist mixed paints in his hand on the palette.

Correct: The artist mixed paints on the palette he held in his hand.

What is the best way to combine each sentence trio?

18. Miss Ling asked if I was ready to give my speech. She asked me before class. My speech is about Gandhi.

(A) Miss Ling asked me before class if I was ready to give my speech about Gandhi.

(B) Miss Ling asked if I was ready to give my speech about Gandhi before class.

(C) Miss Ling asked if I was ready before class to give my Gandhi speech.

---

19. The judge walked past the dogs. The judge was serious. She walked slowly and deliberately.

(A) Seriously, the judge walked slowly past the dogs and deliberately.

(B) The serious judge walked slowly and deliberately past the dogs.

(C) The judge, slowly and deliberately, walked past the serious dogs.

---

20. Monsoons bring cool, dry weather. They bring it in winter. The monsoons are from the north.

(A) Monsoons bring it in winter, the cool, dry north weather.

(B) Monsoons bring cool, dry weather in from the north winter.

(C) Monsoons from the north bring cool, dry weather in winter.

Unit 6
Combining Sentences

21. Platelets help blood clot. They are irregularly shaped bodies. They are colorless.

(A) Platelets, irregularly shaped, colorless bodies, help blood clot.
(B) Irregularly shaped bodies and colorless platelets help blood clot.
(C) Colorless and irregularly shaped bodies help platelets clot blood.

---

22. Plants use the sun's energy. They use the sun's energy to make food. Plants use it to make their own food.

(A) Plants use and make their own food with the sun's energy.
(B) Plants make energy with the sun's food on their own.
(C) Plants use the sun's energy to make their own food.

---

23. The jaws of a snake are flexible. The jaws allow prey to be swallowed. The prey is swallowed whole.

(A) The flexible jaws of prey allow it to be swallowed whole by a snake.
(B) The jaws of a flexible snake allow prey to be swallowed whole.
(C) The flexible jaws of a snake allow prey to be swallowed whole.

---

24. Proteins are nutrients. Our bodies use them to grow. Our bodies use nutrients to heal.

(A) Proteins are nutrients our bodies use to grow and then to heal them.
(B) Proteins are nutrients our bodies use to grow and heal.
(C) Our bodies use them proteins to grow and heal.

---

25. Waterlilies have tough stems. The stems are rubbery. The stems stretch up to ten feet below water.

(A) Waterlilies have tough, rubbery stems that stretch up to ten feet below water.
(B) The stems of waterlilies are tough and rubbery and stretch up to ten feet below water.
(C) Waterlilies have tough stems, are rubbery, and stretch up to ten feet below water.

Unit 7

Combining Sentences

Combining to Make Compound Sentences

Simple sentences that contain related information can be combined to form a compound sentence. Remember that compound sentences are joined by a conjunction *(and, but, or)* and a comma, or they are joined by a semicolon only. Consider what a conjunction means before using it.

Most bat species thrive on insects. +

Many bat species eat at night. =

Most bat species thrive on insects**, and** many eat at night. *OR*

Most bat species thrive on insects**;** many bats eat at night.

Night Pilots

What is the correct way to combine each sentence pair to form a compound sentence?

1. Bats can fly. They are mammals instead of birds.
   (A) Bats can fly, they are mammals instead of birds.
   (B) Bats can fly or they are mammals instead of birds.
   (C) Bats can fly, but they are mammals instead of birds.

2. Bats have existed for millions of years. Fossils show that bats have changed very little.
   (A) Bats have existed for millions of years, fossils show that they have changed very little.
   (B) Bats have existed for millions of years, and fossils show they have changed very little.
   (C) Bats have existed for millions of years or fossils show they have changed very little.

3. We must stop destroying bat habitats. Bats could become extinct.
   (A) We must stop destroying bat habitats, bats could become extinct.
   (B) We must stop destroying bat habitats; or bats could become extinct.
   (C) We must stop destroying bat habitats, or bats could become extinct.

Unit 7
Combining Sentences

Combining to Make Complex Sentences

Sometimes related sentences can be combined to form a complex sentence. A complex sentence has one independent clause and at least one dependent clause. Remember that a dependent clause must begin with a subordinating conjunction, such as *after, although, as, because, before, if, unless, when, where,* and *while.*

We tried the tamales. + We were in Texas. =

We tried the tamales **when** we were in Texas.

A Taste of America

What is the correct way to combine each sentence pair to form a complex sentence?

4. Pumpkin pie will be served. We will get the whipped topping.
(A) Pumpkin pie will be served while we get the whipped topping.
(B) Pumpkin pie will be served, or we will get the whipped topping.
(C) Pumpkin pie will be served, we get the whipped topping.

---

5. We drove through a small town in Maine. We smelled chowder.
(A) We drove through a small town in Maine to smell chowder.
(B) We drove through a small town in Maine, and we smelled chowder.
(C) We drove through a small town in Maine where we smelled chowder.

---

6. Georgia is the Peach State. It is a major producer of the fruit.
(A) Georgia is the Peach State because it is a major producer of the fruit.
(B) Georgia is the Peach State; it is a major producer of the fruit.
(C) Georgia is the Peach State and is a major producer of the fruit.

---

7. You should try Illinois' corn. You visit Illinois.
(A) You should try Illinois' corn and you visit Illinois.
(B) You should try Illinois' corn when you visit Illinois.
(C) You should try Illinois' corn, and you should visit Illinois.

---

8. He tried a Washington red apple. He prefers green apples.
(A) He tried a Washington red apple; he prefers green apples.
(B) He tried a Washington red apple, and he prefers green apples.
(C) He tried a Washington red apple although he prefers green apples.

The Second LAP
Language Activity Pages

A. Exercising Your Skill

You have been learning how to combine sentences, including how to combine various phrases, adjectives, and adverbs. Number your paper from 1 to 8. Read the sentences below. Use a word from the box only once to complete each sentence correctly.

Appositives	Compound	repetition	*and*
Participles	*or*	Complex	appositive

1. Subjects joined by _____ use a verb that agrees with the subject closest to it.
2. Subjects joined by _____ typically use a plural verb form.
3. Combining sentences can help to avoid _____ in writing.
4. _____ are verb forms that can act as adjectives.
5. _____ sentences are made of two or more simple sentences.
6. _____ sentences have one independent clause and at least one dependent clause.
7. _____ are nouns that are located next to other nouns to describe them.
8. An _____ phrase is usually set off by commas.

B. Expanding Your Skill

Number your paper from 1 to 5. Read each sentence below to decide if it is compound or complex. If the sentence is compound, write the letter **D** on your paper. If the sentence is complex, write **X.**

1. Maine is the United States' largest producer of blueberries, since it produces nearly 99% of all blueberries in the country.
2. Maine is the only state name with one syllable, and its only border state is New Hampshire.
3. Maine became the twenty-third state in 1820; its capital is Augusta.
4. Portland, Maine, is the city where poet Henry Wadsworth Longfellow was born.
5. Maine's state insect is the honeybee while its official state bird is the chickadee.

C. Exploring Language

Narrative Writing Number your paper from 1 to 6, and read the paragraph below. Combine each numbered set of sentences by using either an appositive, an appositive phrase, or a participial phrase. The word or words in parentheses after each set of sentences tell which type of word or phrase you should use to combine the sentences.

(1) Karen Hesse wanted to be a writer from an early age. She is the author of 1997's *Out of the Dust* (appositive phrase). (2) Hesse gained confidence to pursue her writing. She was encouraged by her fifth-grade teacher (participial phrase). (3) Hesse's first book was published in 1991. Its title is *Wish on a Unicorn* (appositive). (4) Hesse offers something for many age groups. She is dedicated to quality writing for children and young adults (participial phrase). (5) Hesse has received many awards for her writing. She is the recipient of the impressive Newbery Award for *Out of the Dust* (appositive phrase). (6) *Out of the Dust* was inspired by people's desperate need for rain. It is a unique novel that includes poems and dated entries (participial phrase).

D. Expressing Yourself

Choose one of these activities. When you are finished, give your paper to your teacher.

1. Write at least four sentences to describe a photograph or other image. If possible, choose an image that has an action happening in it. As you write your description, be sure to use adjectives and adverbs correctly. Then combine your sentences following the rules you learned about combining sentences with adjectives and adverbs. Make sure that it is clear in your new sentences what is being described.

2. WORK with a PARTNER Find a partner. You will each take two turns selecting a topic for a total of four different topics. After a topic is said aloud, each of you will write one sentence about the topic. Your sentences must include a prepositional phrase. Then correctly combine your sentence with your partner's. Repeat this process for each topic.

Unit 8

The Sound of Language

Rhyme

There are many ways to make sentences *sound* more interesting. Sometimes a writer chooses certain words because of the way they sound. This can give a different type of movement to a sentence, almost like music or poetry. One writing technique is **internal rhyme**. This means there are words within a sentence or a line that rhyme. Using words with similar or the same sounds can create **rhythm,** which is a pattern of accented (strong) and unaccented (weak) syllables.

The flowers in **bloom** lifted the **room** of its **gloom**.

Choose the sentence that has internal rhyme.

1. **(A)** When I listen to a song, I like to sing along.
   (B) When I listen to a song, I like to sing a lot.
   (C) When I listen to a song, I like to sing with my mom.

2. **(A)** The songwriter hummed and plucked a tune.
   (B) The songwriter hummed and played a tune.
   (C) The songwriter hummed and strummed a tune.

3. **(A)** The melody is not the same as before.
   (B) The melody has a different sound.
   (C) The melody is in a lovely key.

4. **(A)** We do not like the chorus; it has begun to bore us.
   (B) We do not like the chorus; the chorus is too long.
   (C) We do not like the chorus; it has become annoying.

5. **(A)** Justin moves very well on the dance floor.
   (B) Justin moves and grooves on the dance floor.
   (C) Justin moves slowly on the dance floor.

6. **(A)** Roxy always likes the chance to practice.
   (B) Roxy always likes the chance to dance, dance, dance.
   (C) Roxy always dances to her favorite songs.

Unit 8

The Sound of Language

End Rhyme

End rhyme refers to words that rhyme at the end of a sentence or a line. Knowing where end rhyme occurs, it is necessary to have at least two sentences or lines to establish end rhyme.

Check out **Chaz**. He loves that **jazz**!

Choose the sentence that has end rhyme.

7. **(A)** Some singers have a cause. They sing for changes in the country.
   (B) Some singers have a cause. They sing for changes, not applause.
   (C) Some singers have a cause. They sing for changes.

8. **(A)** Alvin listens to the blues. Musicians definitely pay their dues.
   (B) Alvin listens to the blues. He likes it, especially the solos.
   (C) Alvin listens to the blues. He wonders if the stories are real.

9. **(A)** The audience shouted, "Encore!" People knew what that meant.
   (B) The audience shouted, "Encore!" Nobody wanted the night to end.
   (C) The audience shouted, "Encore!" They wanted to hear more.

10. **(A)** The conductor gestured wildly. At the end, he bowed quite slowly.
    (B) The conductor gestured wildly. At the end, he bowed quite mildly.
    (C) The conductor gestured wildly. At the end, he bowed quite quickly.

11. **(A)** Kazuko wanted to share her voice. Opera seemed a logical choice.
    (B) Kazuko wanted to share her voice. Opera seemed to be something she would like.
    (C) Kazuko wanted to share her voice. Opera was one way to achieve her goal.

12. **(A)** Shari would like to perform hip-hop. Her rhyming skills must be sharp.
    (B) Shari would like to perform hip-hop. Her rhyming skills must be tip-top.
    (C) Shari likes hip-hop. Her rhyming skills must be wonderful.

Unit 8

The Sound of Language

Alliteration

Another sound technique in writing is **alliteration**. It is the repetition of the same consonant sound at the beginning of words.

The **b**aby **b**rown **b**umble**b**ee **b**at **b**obs **b**etween the **b**ushes.

Roam the Rain Forest

Choose the sentence that uses alliteration.

13. **(A)** The rain forest is home to many plant and animal species.
(B) A tropical rain forest has species yet to be discovered.
(C) Millions of species wander in this warm, wet wilderness.

---

14. **(A)** The zebra swallowtail caterpillar eats other caterpillars.
(B) Some caterpillars poison their pesky predators for protection.
(C) Caterpillars can have six eye pairs though they do not see well.

---

15. **(A)** Jumping jaguars disappear into the jade jungle.
(B) Like most big cats, jaguars are stealthy hunters.
(C) The okapi resembles both a zebra and a giraffe.

---

16. **(A)** Many rain forest animals are active at night.
(B) A slumped sloth slides so slowly along the stalk.
(C) The ring-tailed lemur is an excellent tree climber.

---

17. **(A)** Tiny tadpoles turn into tree frogs.
(B) If a gecko loses its tail, it can grow a new one.
(C) The slug does not creep at a fast pace.

---

18. **(A)** Gorillas might look fierce, but most are tender creatures.
(B) Gibbons swing across the canopy using branches.
(C) Howler monkeys hoot and holler in their humid habitat.

---

19. **(A)** Plants are vital to the life cycle of the rain forest.
(B) Birds fill the air with tweets, chirps, and other noises.
(C) Lounging lizards lie low on the lush landscape.

Unit 8
The Sound of Language

Assonance

Assonance is the repetition of the same vowel sound in words.

The great **white** str**i**kes with a m**igh**ty b**i**te.

Sea Creatures

Choose the sentence that uses assonance.

20. **(A)** Whales raise their amazing tails.
(B) A newborn blue whale can be the size of an elephant.
(C) Blue whales can weigh over 200 tons.

21. **(A)** Green seaweed is a species we often see.
(B) Sugar kelp is a type of brown seaweed.
(C) Sea lettuce looks like what we use in salads.

22. **(A)** Turtles cover their eggs with sand.
(B) A turtle's front flippers help it steer through water.
(C) Turtles return to the surface for sure.

23. **(A)** The use of long drift nets has been banned.
(B) Swimming into drift nets often kills innocent dolphins.
(C) Whales and seals can also get trapped in the nets.

24. **(A)** Salmon struggle upstream to mate.
(B) Salmon must be strong swimmers.
(C) Salmon hatch in a fast water mass.

25. **(A)** The clown fish is found down around anemones.
(B) An anemone can sting what threatens it.
(C) Clown fish are not hurt by an anemone's sting.

26. **(A)** An electric eel can produce up to a 600-volt shock.
(B) A coral reef is neat and not a piece of the deep sea.
(C) Coral reefs form close to the water's surface.

Unit 8
The Sound of Language

Onomatopoeia

Onomatopoeia is the use of a word to imitate a sound that something makes.

Kernels **popped** out of the pan and **crackled** on the counter.

The word *popped* mimics the sound of something popping, as the word *crackled* mimics the sound of something crackling.

In the Lab

Choose the sentence that has an example of onomatopoeia.

27. **(A)** Glass beakers clanked and clunked in the sink.
(B) Glass beakers fell into a pile in the sink.

28. **(A)** The solution made strange sounds when stirred.
(B) The solution hissed and sizzled when stirred.

29. **(A)** The flame became weak and then went out.
(B) The flame fluttered and fizzled.

30. **(A)** Snap your safety goggles into place.
(B) Put on the safety goggles that fit.

31. **(A)** The mouse made small sounds and rapid movements as it went through the maze.
(B) The mouse squeaked, twitched, and zipped as it finished the maze.

32. **(A)** We carefully crushed the crystals in a dish.
(B) We broke the crystals into pieces in a dish.

33. **(A)** The chemical mixture boomed and puffed.
(B) The mixture produced a noise and a smoky cloud.

34. **(A)** Students had trouble breathing, so they left the room.
(B) Wheezing and whimpering, students left the lab.

Unit 8
The Sound of Language

Repetition

Sometimes, in special instances such as poetry and storytelling, a writer wants to repeat himself or herself. **Repetition** can be a positive writing element when it is intended or used for effect. It can add drama or emphasis to writing. Repeated words and phrases get a reader's attention.

The hot air balloon lifted **up, up,** and away!

Tick tock, tick tock, time **ticked** and **tocked** off the clock.

Choose the sentence that uses repetition.

35. **(A)** I cannot stop looking at the kite in the sky.
(B) I cannot stop looking at the blue, blue sky.

____

36. **(A)** Toby asked himself, "Why did this happen now?"
(B) Toby asked himself, "Why now? Why now?"

____

37. **(A)** She loves to spend time at the gym; she even studies there.
(B) She works at the gym, exercises at the gym, and studies at the gym; she just loves the gym!

____

38. **(A)** Workers dug deeper and deeper looking for the busted pipe.
(B) Workers kept on digging to look for the broken pipe.

____

39. **(A)** I cannot bear to leave, but I cannot bear to stay.
(B) I do not want to leave, and I should not stay.

____

40. **(A)** Every day it is the same routine.
(B) Day after day after day, we get up, get dressed, and get going.

____

41. **(A)** The tall, brawny cowboy got on his tall, brawny horse.
(B) The tall cowboy got on his brown horse.

____

42. **(A)** Jasper is the most loyal friend I have ever known.
(B) Jasper is a true friend, the truest friend I know.

Unit 9

Sentence Fluency

It is good to avoid too many short sentences or too many long sentences when writing. Using a variety of sentence lengths and types sounds better and adds interest to your work. **Sentence fluency** refers to making sure sentences flow from one to the next in a smooth and logical way. Transition words can help writers move easily from one sentence to another. They indicate time, location, or order. Some examples are *at, below, near, after, today, when, before, during,* and *finally.*

Good: People have been visiting Greece for centuries. They have gone to see ancient remains. Greek temples and artwork are popular and magnificent. These attractions are found throughout Greece. Tourists also go to Greece because it has superb resorts.

Better: People have been visiting Greece for centuries, mostly to view ancient remains. Found throughout the country, magnificent Greek temples and artwork are popular attractions. Today, many tourists also spend time in Greece because of its superb resorts.

Choose the best example of sentence fluency.

1. **(A)** Has anyone ever called you a *diphyodont?* A diphyodont is a being that develops two sets of teeth in its lifetime. The *deciduous teeth,* or baby teeth, start falling or coming out around the age of six. They are replaced by a larger set known simply as *permanent teeth.*

   (B) Has anyone ever called you a *diphyodont,* which is a being that develops two sets of teeth in its lifetime? The *deciduous teeth,* or baby teeth, start falling or coming out around the age of six. Then they are replaced by a larger set of what can simply be called *permanent teeth.*

   (C) Has anyone ever called you a *diphyodont?* A diphyodont is a being that develops two sets of teeth in its lifetime. The *deciduous teeth* start falling or coming out around the age of six. This set of teeth is also called baby teeth. Then they are replaced by a larger set of teeth. These are known simply as *permanent teeth.*

2. **(A)** An endangered species is close to extinction. It is close to dying out completely. Many plant species throughout the world are endangered. Many animal species are endangered too. The main reason is habitat destruction.

   (B) An endangered species is one that is close to extinction, or dying out completely. Many plant and animal species throughout the world are endangered, and the main reason for this is the destruction of their habitats.

   (C) When a species is endangered, it is close to extinction or dying out completely. Many plant and animal species throughout the world are endangered. The main reason a species becomes endangered is habitat destruction.

3. **(A)** Damon walked down the last step of the bus, and he was feeling happy, but suddenly his mood changed. He realized he did not have his house key. How would he get into his family's house? He remembered something his parents said. Then Damon looked in a secret, concealed spot and with luck found a spare key.

   (B) Damon was on the last step. He walked down off the bus. He was feeling good. Suddenly, his mood changed. He realized he did not have his house key. How would he get in? Then Damon remembered something. He looked in a secret, concealed spot to find the spare key.

   (C) Damon walked down the last step of the bus. He was feeling happy. Suddenly, his mood changed as he realized he did not have his house key. How would he get into his family's house? Then he remembered something his parents had said. Damon looked in a secret, concealed spot. Luckily, there was a spare key!

Unit 9
Sentence Fluency

Choose the best example of sentence fluency.

4. **(A)** A windmill turns wind into useful energy. It stands tall atop a typically rounded structure with blades similar to a ceiling fan. Historians believe this machine was developed in ancient times. Windmills from the 1500s to the 1900s helped with a variety of chores. A windmill's energy could be used to pump water, saw wood, and press oil from seeds for household purposes.

   (B) A windmill turns wind into useful energy. It stands tall, can be a rounded structure, and has blades like a ceiling fan. Historians believe this machine came from ancient times. Later windmills helped with a variety of chores. They pumped water. They sawed wood. They pressed oil from seeds for household purposes.

5. **(A)** Many people are fascinated by Mars because out of all the planets in our solar system, Mars most closely resembles Earth. Scientists found evidence that there was water on Mars. Water is necessary for living organisms. This discovery was especially exciting.

   (B) Many people are fascinated by Mars. Of all the planets in our solar system, Mars most closely resembles Earth. Not long ago, scientists found evidence of water on Mars. Because water is necessary for living organisms, this discovery was especially exciting.

6. **(A)** The gray fox has a varied diet. The main part of its diet is smaller mammals, such as mice and rabbits. Gray foxes will also snack on corn, apples, nuts, and berries. In summer and fall, they have been known to feast on large helpings of crickets and grasshoppers.

   (B) The gray fox has a varied diet. The main part of its diet is smaller mammals. It eats smaller mammals such as mice and rabbits. Gray foxes will also snack on other things. They eat corn, apples, nuts, and berries. In summer and fall, the gray fox enjoys a lot of crickets. It also eats a lot of grasshoppers.

7. **(A)** An octopus has an amazing ability. It can change. It can rapidly change color. Some can change shape. The mimic octopus can imitate fish. It can also imitate giant crabs and snakes.

   (B) An octopus has an amazing ability to change. For example, it can rapidly change color to blend in with its surroundings. Some octopuses can change shape. The mimic octopus can imitate fish, giant crabs, and snakes.

8. **(A)** You can use the "Three *R*s" of conservation. Use them when buying groceries. First, *Reduce* by buying products with less packaging. Next, you can *Reuse.* Take a canvas bag to the store. Use it to transfer items home. Finally, you can *Recycle* glass, paper, and plastic. Once emptied, some metal containers are recyclable too.

   (B) Use the "Three *R*s" of conservation when buying groceries. First, *Reduce* by buying products with less packaging. Next, *Reuse* by using a canvas bag to transfer items home from the store. Finally, *Recycle* glass, paper, plastic, and appropriate metal containers once emptied.

9. **(A)** In Australia's Outback, a huge desert region, many people live isolated from others. It is too difficult for a doctor to see patients in this territory by driving. That is why the Royal Flying Doctor Service was established. Now people of the Outback are cared for sooner.

   (B) In Australia's Outback, which is a huge desert region, many people live isolated from others, and it is difficult for a doctor to see patients in this territory by taking a car from place to place. For quicker service, the Royal Flying Doctor Service was established.

10. **(A)** Pasta is a kind of dough. It is made with wheat flour and water. These ingredients are not appetizing to everyone, but pasta has become very popular. It is made in many different flavors. Pasta shapes vary. It can be filled with cheese and/or meat. Vegetables can be filling too.

    (B) Pasta starts as dough made with wheat flour and water. Although these simple ingredients may not sound appetizing, pasta has become an extremely popular food. Pasta is made in different flavors and shapes and can have cheese, meat, and/or vegetable filling.

The Third LAP
Language Activity Pages

A. Exercising Your Skill

You have been learning about techniques that can help you share words and writing in fun, interesting ways. You have also learned what sentence fluency refers to and how to achieve it. Number your paper from 1 to 10. Read each sentence below to decide if it is true or false. If a sentence is true, write the letter **T** on your paper. If a sentence is false, write the letter **F** on your paper.

1. Internal rhyme occurs within more than one word of a line or a sentence.
2. End rhyme occurs in the first words of two lines or sentences.
3. Rhythm refers to a pattern of strong and weak syllables when similar-sounding words are used together.
4. Assonance is the repetition of the same consonant sound at the beginning of words.
5. Alliteration is the repetition of the same vowel sound in words.
6. Repetition is a positive writing element when it is used for effect.
7. Words that are repeated can grab the attention of readers.
8. Sentence fluency means avoiding a lot of short or long sentences.
9. Transition words can show time, location, or order.
10. Onomatopoeia is the use of a word to mimic a sound something makes.

B. Expanding Your Skill

Number your paper from 1 to 6. Read the examples below. Choose the correct technique from the box to match its word or writing example. Write the letter of the technique on your paper.

(A) alliteration	**(B)** assonance	**(C)** end rhyme
(D) internal rhyme	**(E)** onomatopoeia	**(F)** repetition

1. The chimney flue was cleaned by Sue, and now the bill is due.
2. Zach the zookeeper zoomed over to Zanzibar to see about a zebra.
3. Over steps, over the rug, over chairs, over the table leapt the cat.
4. I sat on a can that was under a map that used to be on the dash.
5. The jumping fish whizzed and splished in its tank.
6. The money has been spent. Do you know where it went?

C. Exploring Language

Poetry Number your paper from 1 to 6. Read the poem below. There is one example of each sound-of-language technique. For each technique, write the letter of each line that matches it. Remember that two lines are needed for end rhyme.

(A) Swinging in the sweaty swamp,

(B) the baboon learned soon it was noon.

(C) The sun in the sky

(D) sizzled

(E) as the oldest of high

(F) trees blew in the breeze with ease.

(G) Away the baboon from vine to vine to vine.

Techniques	**Lines**
1. Internal Rhyme	_____
2. End Rhyme	_____
3. Alliteration	_____
4. Assonance	_____
5. Onomatopoeia	_____
6. Repetition	_____

D. Expressing Yourself

Choose one of these activities. When you are finished, give your paper to your teacher.

1. Write a brief "How To" or a demonstration speech. For example, you might explain how to make a sandwich, wash a car, or prepare a camera to take photographs. Make sure to consider your sentence fluency. Include transition words to clearly outline the order in which the steps of the process are to be completed.

2. WORK with a PARTNER Find a partner, and select a topic for a brief descriptive paragraph. For example, describe a gadget, an animal, a place, or an event. Work together to write the description. When you are done, take time to improve the sentence fluency of the paragraph. Use transition words if they are helpful to your topic and have not been used yet.

Unit 10

Parallelism

Parallelism refers to making parts of a sentence parallel, or match, in form. Follow the rules below when you write sentences.

- Verbs that have the same subject must be in the same tense and form.
  Not Parallel: Brazil mines and produced stunning emeralds.
  Parallel: Brazil **mines** and **produces** stunning emeralds.
- Adverbs that modify the same verb must have the same level of comparison. For example, if one adverb ends with *-ly,* the other adverb or adverbs must also end with *-ly.*
  Not Parallel: Some people search far and wider for a perfect gem.
  Parallel: Some people search **far** and **wide** for a perfect gem.
- Adjectives that describe the same noun must have the same level of comparison. For example, if one adjective ends with *-est,* the other adjective or adjectives must also end with *-est.*
  Not Parallel: No emeralds are clearer or brightest than Colombia's.
  Parallel: No emeralds are **clearer** or **brighter** than Colombia's.

Are the underlined words in the correct form?

Gorgeous Green Gems

An emerald is a gemstone that can display a (1) deeper and brilliant shade of green. The emerald has a lengthy and (2) livelier history dating back to early Egypt. Pharaohs (3) treasured the gems and often mined them greedily. Museums throughout the world display some of the finest and (4) lovely emerald collections. One collection includes a (5) carefully and beautifully crafted emerald tiara, which once belonged to an empress.

1. **(A)** Yes **(B)** No, change to *deep*

2. **(A)** Yes **(B)** No, change to *lively*

3. **(A)** Yes **(B)** No, change to *were treasuring*

4. **(A)** Yes **(B)** No, change to *loveliest*

5. **(A)** Yes **(B)** No, change to *careful*

Unit 10
Parallelism

The Hope Diamond

The Hope Diamond is the most popular and perhaps the **(6)** more impressive gem on display at the Smithsonian. It has an intense, soothing blue color, unlike the most common type of diamond, which **(7)** has a whitish color due to its clarity. The **(8)** rarest and radiant Hope Diamond weighs 45.52 carats. More than a billion years ago, the diamond was formed far below Earth's surface and then **(9)** was forced out when a volcano erupted. Smithsonian visitors can watch the Hope Diamond turn slowly and **(10)** most elegantly.

6. **(A)** Yes **(B)** No, change to *most impressive*

7. **(A)** Yes **(B)** No, change to *had*

8. **(A)** Yes **(B)** No, change to *rare*

9. **(A)** Yes **(B)** No, change to *is forced*

10. **(A)** Yes **(B)** No, change to *elegantly*

What Are Baobabs?

Baobabs are African trees; they can be both **(11)** regal and eerie in appearance. A baobab's trunk can grow up to eighty feet around and **(12)** is living up to a few thousand years! It has been noted that baobab branches look much like roots, sprawling extensively and **(13)** wildly. When in season, baobabs **(14)** have produced and offer a fruit protected by a woody shell covered with short, velvety hairs. The pulp of the fruit can be turned into a **(15)** tasty and nutritious food or drink.

11. **(A)** Yes **(B)** No, change to *more regal*

12. **(A)** Yes **(B)** No, change to *can live*

13. **(A)** Yes **(B)** No, change to *more wildly*

14. **(A)** Yes **(B)** No, change to *produce*

15. **(A)** Yes **(B)** No, change to *tastier*

Unit 10

Parallelism

Are the underlined words in the correct form?

Emma Edmonds

Canada was the birthplace of Emma Edwards, but she **(16)** felt a strong connection to the United States. Edmonds was a courageous, **(17)** younger woman who joined the Union Army during America's Civil War. Working as a spy, Edmonds cleverly and **(18)** brave acquired information from Confederate soldiers. She wore different and **(19)** sneaky disguises to infiltrate the enemy's camp. Sometimes Edmonds dressed as an escaped male slave or **(20)** posed as a peddler. The most startling part of Edmonds' story is that she had to pretend to be a man her entire army career. So, at times, she was a woman pretending to be a man pretending to be a woman!

16. **(A)** Yes **(B)** No, change to *feels*

17. **(A)** Yes **(B)** No, change to *young*

18. **(A)** Yes **(B)** No, change to *bravely*

19. **(A)** Yes **(B)** No, change to *sneakier*

20. **(A)** Yes **(B)** No, change to *poses*

The Alps

Located in south-central Europe, the Alps span nearly 700 miles and **(21)** enhance the scenery of ten countries. Including slopes in Switzerland and Italy, expert skiers conquer the Alps skillfully and **(22)** frequently. Mont Blanc in France is the **(23)** highest, grandest point of the Alps. It **(24)** stood, or measures, 15,771 feet.

21. **(A)** Yes **(B)** No, change to *enhanced*

22. **(A)** Yes **(B)** No, change to *more frequently*

23. **(A)** Yes **(B)** No, change to *higher*

24. **(A)** Yes **(B)** No, change to *stands*

Unit 10
Parallelism

Frederick Douglass

In historic times of slavery in America, teaching slaves to read was illegal and **(25)** <u>riskier</u>. However, Frederick Douglass found ways to learn and **(26)** <u>believed</u> that reading and writing could lead him to freedom. In fact, Douglass would become known near and **(27)** <u>farther</u> for his eloquence. After he daringly and **(28)** <u>most narrowly</u> escaped from slavery, Douglass was a leader in the movement to abolish slavery. He wrote and **(29)** <u>did publish</u> *The North Star,* a newspaper that promoted freedom for all people. As a public speaker, Douglass influenced his listeners with the **(30)** <u>truest</u> and noblest of speeches.

25. **(A)** Yes **(B)** No, change to *risky*

26. **(A)** Yes **(B)** No, change to *was believing*

27. **(A)** Yes **(B)** No, change to *far*

28. **(A)** Yes **(B)** No, change to *narrowly*

29. **(A)** Yes **(B)** No, change to *published*

30. **(A)** Yes **(B)** No, change to *truer*

The Taj Mahal

The Taj Mahal in India exists as history's greatest and **(31)** <u>bolder</u> memorial to love. In the year 1612, Mumtaz Mahal and Shah Jehan were deeply in love and **(32)** <u>decide</u> to marry. Becoming empress upon their marriage, Mumtaz **(33)** <u>accompanied</u> and advised her husband well. After her death in 1630, Shah Jehan decided to immortalize their love and **(34)** <u>began</u> to build the Taj Mahal. It is a palace and a shrine designed for the adoration of one woman.

31. **(A)** Yes **(B)** No, change to *boldest*

32. **(A)** Yes **(B)** No, change to *decided*

33. **(A)** Yes **(B)** No, change to *was accompanying*

34. **(A)** Yes **(B)** No, change to *begins*

Unit 11

Sentence Problems

With so many different types of sentences, it is not difficult to forget something or make a mistake. One kind of error is writing a **fragment,** which is a group of words written as a sentence but is missing its subject, predicate, or both. A fragment is incorrect and does *not* express a complete thought.

Without a subject: Are helpful to record data.

Without a predicate: Charts and graphs for scientific research.

Without both: Data using charts and graphs.

Correct: Scientific data can be recorded on charts and graphs.

Scientific Strategy

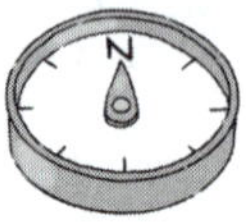

Is each group of words a complete sentence or a fragment?

1. Using an organized approach to solving a problem.
   (A) Sentence
   (B) Fragment

2. The first step is identifying a question or a problem.
   (A) Sentence
   (B) Fragment

3. A hypothesis is based on previous knowledge and observations.
   (A) Sentence
   (B) Fragment

4. Has to be something you can test through investigation.
   (A) Sentence
   (B) Fragment

5. Analyzing data by looking for patterns, and thinking critically about what they mean.
   (A) Sentence
   (B) Fragment

6. Drawing a conclusion involves making judgments.
   (A) Sentence
   (B) Fragment

Unit 11
Sentence Problems

The Territory of the Buffalo

7. Roamed the open land on horseback, following and hunting buffalo.
   (A) Sentence
   (B) Fragment

8. Plains Indians depended on the woolly beasts, which provided food and shelter.
   (A) Sentence
   (B) Fragment

9. No part of the buffalo went to waste; their bones were shaped into tools, including knives and fishhooks.
   (A) Sentence
   (B) Fragment

10. Would trade buffalo hides and beaver skins for other goods.
    (A) Sentence
    (B) Fragment

11. After the Civil War, railroads hired hunters to kill buffalo.
    (A) Sentence
    (B) Fragment

12. In order to feed the railroad workers and keep herds of buffalo from blocking the tracks.
    (A) Sentence
    (B) Fragment

13. In just a few years, white people killed more than nine million buffalo.
    (A) Sentence
    (B) Fragment

14. Destroying the buffalo and changing the Plains Indians' way of life forever.
    (A) Sentence
    (B) Fragment

Unit 11

Sentence Problems

Another writing mistake is a **run-on sentence.** This occurs when two or more sentences are incorrectly written as one sentence. To fix this problem, write the run-on sentences separately, or combine them with a comma and a conjunction (*and, but, or*) or a semicolon only.

Run-on: Metro Park was built in 2000 it has areas for skateboarding and in-line skating.

Correct: Metro Park was built in 2000; it has areas for skateboarding and in-line skating.

Extreme Fun

Is each sentence a run-on sentence?

15. With hundreds of skateboard parks in the United States, one might be near you!
(A) Yes **(B)** No

---

16. Features at the parks include quarter pipes, banks, and rails they add to the excitement.
(A) Yes **(B)** No

---

17. Some skating parks are indoors some are outdoors.
(A) Yes **(B)** No

---

18. Helmets, knee pads, and elbow pads are recommended for the skaters' protection.
(A) Yes **(B)** No

---

19. Some parks offer lessons to beginning skaters or skaters who want to learn new tricks.
(A) Yes **(B)** No

---

20. Professional skateboarders have an annual competition it can be attended in person or seen on television.
(A) Yes **(B)** No

Millions of Years

21. India was once a separate continent today it is part of Asia.
(A) Yes
(B) No

---

22. India moved toward Asia the two landmasses attached.
(A) Yes
(B) No

---

23. The force of the continents' collision pushed up the earth, forming the world's highest mountain range.
(A) Yes
(B) No

---

24. The Himalayas are a chain of mountains many of the peaks are more than 25,000 feet high.
(A) Yes
(B) No

---

25. Mt. Everest, the world's highest peak, is in the Himalayas.
(A) Yes
(B) No

---

26. Fossils of shellfish, which live in the ocean, have been found near the top of Mt. Everest.
(A) Yes
(B) No

---

27. This shows that part of the ocean floor was pushed many thousands of feet upward while the Himalayas were forming.
(A) Yes
(B) No

---

28. Breathtaking events happen over time I wonder what might happen in another million years!
(A) Yes
(B) No

Unit 11

Sentence Problems

A pronoun can take the place of a noun. The noun a pronoun replaces is called its **antecedent**. When you use a pronoun to replace a noun, it must be clear which noun the pronoun is replacing. If it is not clear, the reader may get confused.

- A sentence is unclear if a pronoun could refer to more than one noun. Sometimes you must repeat a noun or rewrite a sentence to avoid confusion.

  Mom drove Lydia to the store. She needed a pair of gloves. (It is not clear if *She* refers to *Mom* or to *Lydia.*)

  Mom drove Lydia to the store. **Lydia** needed a pair of gloves.

Is it clear which noun each underlined pronoun replaces?

29. Todd sat with Ian at lunch. He had an egg salad sandwich.
(A) It is clear.
(B) It is not clear.

30. Augusto's grandparents are from Chile. They often talk to him about their home country.
(A) It is clear.
(B) It is not clear.

31. Maya joined Nellie at the park. She wanted to play baseball.
(A) It is clear.
(B) It is not clear.

32. The Carters met the Smiths at the restaurant. They were tired.
(A) It is clear.
(B) It is not clear.

33. Sugi collects books about the American Revolution. She thinks it is an interesting subject.
(A) It is clear.
(B) It is not clear.

34. The walking stick crawled up the fence. It was long.
(A) It is clear.
(B) It is not clear.

Unit 11
Sentence Problems

35. The bakers are serving the customers. They are excited about the fresh loaves of sourdough bread.
(A) It is clear.
(B) It is not clear.

---

36. A falcon pursued a chipmunk. It was near the field in which it lives.
(A) It is clear.
(B) It is not clear.

---

37. Tamera and Gillian are working on a science project. They are learning about friction.
(A) It is clear.
(B) It is not clear.

---

38. Hector's parents own two Chihuahuas. They do not like to run.
(A) It is clear.
(B) It is not clear.

---

39. Todd cannot wait to listen to his new album. It is by the band Rockets and Sockets.
(A) It is clear.
(B) It is not clear.

---

40. Lucy Maud Montgomery wrote a famous book about a character named Anne. She was an orphan.
(A) It is clear.
(B) It is not clear.

---

41. Geologists are scientists who study a planet's history through rocks. They are fascinating.
(A) It is clear.
(B) It is not clear.

---

42. The Rocky Mountains have jagged peaks. They are located partly in Colorado.
(A) It is clear.
(B) It is not clear.

Unit 12
Expanding Sentences

Adding details to sentences can help make writing more interesting and less choppy. Adding a participial phrase is one way to expand a sentence. A participial phrase begins with an *-ed* or an *-ing* verb form and cannot stand alone.

The books belong to the library. →

The books **sitting on the top shelf** belong to the library.

The Local Library

Which sentence has been correctly expanded to include a participial phrase?

1. I could not wait to read more.

(A) I could not wait to read more of the amazing story.
(B) Amazed by the story, I could not wait to read more.
(C) Amazingly, I could not wait to read more of the story.

2. These books cannot be checked out.

(A) These books, in the reference section, cannot be checked out.
(B) These books cannot be checked out because they are in the reference section.
(C) These books located in the reference section cannot be checked out.

3. The librarian suggested some books.

(A) The librarian made some helpful suggestions about books.
(B) The librarian helping with our project suggested some books.
(C) The librarian suggested that we find other books.

4. I found the book I wanted.

(A) Looking at the call numbers, I found the book I wanted.
(B) I looked at the call numbers to find the book I wanted.
(C) Looking at the call numbers helped me find the book.

5. The man is the newest librarian.

(A) The man is the newest librarian to shelve books and movies.
(B) The man shelving books and movies is the newest librarian.
(C) The newest librarian is the man who shelves books and movies.

Unit 12

Expanding Sentences

Another way to expand sentences is to add an appositive or an appositive phrase. An appositive is a noun that is located next to another noun which it describes. An appositive phrase acts like an appositive but includes the other words that modify the appositive.

Appositive: England's busiest city, **London,** is also a port.

Appositive Phrase: Westminster, **an abbey where royalty is crowned,** is in London.

Around the World

Which sentence has been correctly expanded to include an appositive or an appositive phrase?

6. The home of the Eiffel Tower is in France.
   (A) Paris, France, has the Eiffel Tower.
   (B) Paris is the home of the Eiffel Tower.
   (C) The home of the Eiffel Tower, Paris, is in France.

7. Australia's most famous building is unique.
   (A) Australia's most famous building, the Sydney Opera House, is unique.
   (B) Australia's most famous building is unique, the Sydney Opera House.
   (C) The Sydney Opera House is Australia's most famous, unique building.

8. Sunflowers produce seeds that make oil.
   (A) Sunflowers, a vital crop in the Ukraine, produce seeds that make oil.
   (B) Sunflowers growing in the Ukraine produce seeds that make oil.
   (C) Sunflower crops, vital in the Ukraine, produce seeds that make oil.

9. The yak is a central part of life in Tibet.
   (A) The yak is a kind of ox, which is a central part of life in Tibet.
   (B) The yak, a kind of ox, is a central part of life in Tibet.
   (C) As a central part of life in Tibet, the yak is a kind of ox.

10. The world's largest desert was fertile thousands of years ago.
    (A) The world's largest desert, the Sahara, was fertile thousands of years ago.
    (B) As the world's largest desert, the Sahara was fertile thousands of years ago.
    (C) Thousands of years ago the Sahara Desert, the largest, was fertile.

The Last LAP
Language Activity Pages

A. Exercising Your Skill

You have been learning about different types of sentence problems. You have also learned how to use participial phrases, appositives, and appositive phrases to expand sentences. Number your paper from 1 to 8. Read each sentence below to decide if it is true or false. If a sentence is true, write the letter **T** on your paper. If a sentence is false, write the letter **F** on your paper.

1. Parallelism refers to making parts of a sentence match in form.
2. Parallelism does not apply to adverbs or adjectives.
3. A fragment does not express a complete thought.
4. A run-on occurs when two or more sentences are incorrectly written as one sentence.
5. A run-on sentence can be corrected by identifying the mistakes and then writing two separate sentences.
6. An antecedent is the noun a pronoun replaces in a sentence.
7. Appositive phrases include the appositive and its modifiers.
8. Participial phrases can stand alone.

B. Expanding Your Skill

Number your paper from 1 to 8. Carefully read the sentences below. Each underlined word is not written in the form it should be. Write the correct form of each word on your paper.

1. Kin Yee worries about and <u>dreading</u> his math test on fractions.
2. The gym teacher <u>explains</u> and demonstrated the game.
3. Carson needs a <u>quieter</u> and large area to do his homework.
4. As I expected, Kammy <u>easier</u> and confidently won the contest.
5. Omar was practicing and <u>edit</u> his speech.
6. The art teacher helps us to <u>firing</u> and glaze our pottery.
7. The relieved and <u>happiest</u> students put down their pencils.
8. While observing, Geraldo silently and <u>most thoroughly</u> took notes.

C. Exploring Language

Personal Writing Number your paper from 1 to 8. Read the journal entry below. Each sentence has an error. The errors could be fragments or run-ons. There are also a few pronouns that do not clearly refer to their antecedents. If the sentence error is a fragment, write the letter **G** on your paper. If the sentence error is a run-on, write the letter **R.** If there is an unclear antecedent in the sentence, write the letter **U.**

Skiing and snowboarding last weekend with Uncle Doug. A weekend I will never forget. The slopes were not crowded when we arrived we were thrilled! The sun shined down on the snow; it was very bright. The snow had the perfect texture we glided on it as if we were professional athletes. Felt like flying! Uncle Doug went with Brian to ski the black diamonds because he likes the most challenging ski courses. Only two of us attempted to snowboard that was the most fun of all!

D. Expressing Yourself

Choose one of these activities. When you are finished, give your paper to your teacher.

1. Think of a weekend journey you have taken with family or friends. Write a brief paragraph to describe where you went, who went with you, what the experience was, and how you felt about it. Select four of your sentences to correctly expand using participial phrases. For example, *The tent did not get that wet* could be expanded into *The tent* ***placed under the tree's canopy*** *did not get that wet.*

2. WORK with a PARTNER Find a partner, and write a brief adventure story together. Select an exotic or a foreign place that you have heard of, read about, or would like to visit. Think of specific countries and cities to include in your story. You might want to use an atlas, an almanac, or other geographic reference to get ideas. When the story is done, pick four of your sentences to correctly expand using appositives and appositive phrases. Try to add two of each. For example, *Monaco,* ***a gorgeous principality,*** *has an annual Grand Prix race,* and *Monaco,* ***a gorgeous principality on the Mediterranean coast of France,*** *has an annual Grand Prix race.*

SENTENCES Scope and Sequence • *Specific Skill Series for Language Arts*

Unit/Level	Level A	Level B	Level C	Level D	Level E	Level F	Level G	Level H
Unit 1	Building Sentences	Building Sentences	Building Sentences	Building Sentences	Building Sentences	Building Sentences	Building Sentences	Building Sentences
Unit 2	Building Sentences	Building Sentences	Building Sentences	Building Sentences	Building Sentences	Building Sentences	Combining Sentences	Combining Sentences
Unit 3	Building Sentences	Building Sentences	Building Sentences	Building Sentences	Building Sentences	Building Sentences	Combining Sentences	Combining Sentences
Unit 4	Building Sentences	Building Sentences	Building Sentences	Building Sentences	Building Sentences	Building Sentences	The Sound of Language	The Sound of Language
Unit 5	Building Sentences	Combining Sentences	Building Sentences	Building Sentences	Combining Sentences	Combining Sentences	Sentence Fluency	Sentence Fluency
Unit 6	Combining Sentences	Combining Sentences	Building Sentences	Building Sentences	Combining Sentences	Combining Sentences	Parallelism	Parallelism
Unit 7	Combining Sentences	Correct Word Order in a Sentence	Combining Sentences	Combining Sentences	Combining Sentences	The Sound of Language	Parallelism	Parallelism
Unit 8	Putting Words in the Correct Order	Parallelism	Combining Sentences	Combining Sentences	The Sound of Language	Sentence Fluency	Sentence Problems	Sentence Problems
Unit 9	Agreement with Verbs and Adjectives	Sentence Problems	Combining Sentences	Combining Sentences	Sentence Fluency	Parallelism	Sentence Problems	Sentence Problems
Unit 10	Sentence Problems	Sentence Problems	Combining Sentences	Correct Word Order	Parallelism	Sentence Problems	Expanding Sentences	Expanding Sentences
Unit 11	Adding Prepositional Phrases	Adding Prepositional Phrases	Combining Sentences	The Sound of Language	Sentence Problems	Expanding Sentences	Diagramming Sentences	Diagramming Sentences
Unit 12			Correct Word Order	Sentence Fluency	Expanding Sentences			
Unit 13			Parallelism	Parallelism				
Unit 14			Sentence Fluency	Sentence Problems				
Unit 15			Sentence Problems	Sentence Problems				
Unit 16			Sentence Problems	Sentence Problems				